DISCARDED

A Note to Parents and Teachers

Kids can imagine, kids can laugh and kids can learn to read with this exciting new series of first readers. Each book in the Kids Can Read series has been especially written, illustrated and designed for beginning readers. Humorous, easy-to-read stories, appealing characters and topics, and engaging illustrations make for books that kids will want to read over and over again.

To make selecting a book easy for kids, parents and teachers, the Kids Can Read series offers three levels based on different reading abilities:

Level 1: Kids Can Start to Read

Short stories, simple sentences, easy vocabulary, lots of repetition and visual clues for kids just beginning to read.

Level 2: Kids Can Read with Help

Longer stories, varied sentences, increased vocabulary, some repetition and visual clues for kids who have some reading skills, but may need a little help.

Level 3: Kids Can Read Alone

More challenging topics, more complex sentences, advanced vocabulary, language play, minimal repetition and visual clues for kids who are reading by themselves.

With the Kids Can Read series, kids can enter a new and exciting world of reading!

Looking at Bears

Written by Deborah Hodge

Illustrated by Pat Stephens

Kids Can Press

I spy ...

Look in this book.

Can you find these pictures?

 A jumping fish

 A baby bear in a tree

 A bear eating leaves

Bears

Bears are big animals.

They are very strong.

Bears have long claws and sharp teeth.

Kinds of bears

There are many kinds of bears.
Here are three kinds.

Black bear

Black bears are big.
They can grow to be as long as a bathtub.

Grizzly bear

Grizzly bears are bigger than black bears.

Polar bear

Polar bears are the biggest bears of all.

Where bears live

Bears live in many places.

Polar bears live in the north.
They like to live where it is very cold.

Black bear

Black bears live in forests.

Grizzly bears live in forests and mountains.

They try to stay far away from people.

Bear bodies

Each part of a bear's body has a special job to do.

Fur
Fur helps bears stay warm in winter.

Claws
Sharp claws are good for digging.

Nose
Bears use their noses to help them find food.

Teeth
Bears have sharp teeth for eating meat.

What bears eat

Bears eat plants and animals.

This polar bear is waiting to catch a seal.
Seals swim in the water under the ice.

This black bear likes to eat the honey
that bees make.

This grizzly bear is digging.
It wants to snack on some roots.

How bears move

Most of the time,
bears walk on all four feet.
Sometimes they stand up
on their back legs.

All bears can swim.
Polar bears swim fast and far.

Sharp claws help black bears climb trees.

Grizzly bears can run much faster
than you can!

Bear homes

A home for a bear is called a den.

Bears make dens when winter comes.

A polar bear makes a den
by digging in snow.
Later she will have her babies there.

A black bear makes a den
under tree roots or under a bush.

A grizzly bear digs its den
in the side of a hill.

Winter sleep

In winter, there is not much food
for black bears and grizzly bears.
They fall asleep inside winter dens.
The bears will sleep until
spring comes.

Polar bears can find food all winter long.
Only polar bear mothers go into dens.

18

Black bear

Baby bears

Baby bears are called cubs.

New cubs don't have fur.

Their mother's fur keeps them warm.

Polar bear and cubs

21

How bears learn

By spring, the cubs are much bigger.
They are furry and they love to play!

Cubs learn by watching their mother.
They learn to find food and stay safe.

Black bear and cubs

Bears and people

Most bears try to stay away
from people.
People do not always
stay away from bears.

People sometimes build homes and roads
in places where bears live.
People may cut down the trees
in a forest where bears live.

Then the bears must look for
a new place to live.

Bears around the world

There are other kinds of bears
in places around the world.

This is a sun bear.
It is the smallest kind of bear.
Sun bears like to eat bugs.

This is a sloth bear with her cub.
Sloth bear mothers carry their cubs
on their backs.

This is a panda bear.

It is snacking on leaves.

Panda bears eat all day long.

Bear tracks

An animal footprint is called a track.
Here are some bear tracks.

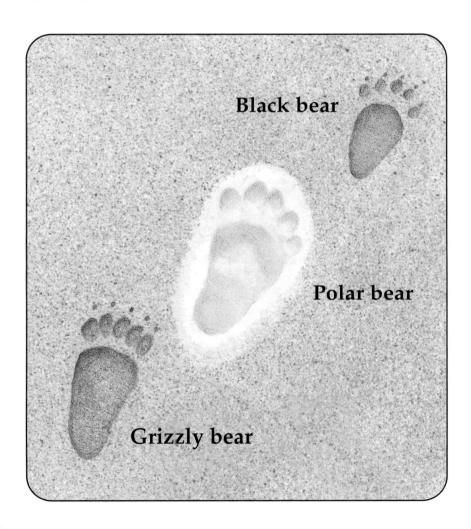

Black bear

Polar bear

Grizzly bear

Real bear tracks are much bigger
than these pictures.

What bear am I?

See if you can answer these bear riddles.

1. I am white.
    I like to live where it is very cold.
    What bear am I?

2. I like to live near mountains.

   I dig my den in the side of a hill.

   What bear am I?

3. I live in the forest.

   There is a color in my name.

   What bear am I?

Answers: 1. Polar bear   2. Grizzly bear   3. Black bear

Kids Can Read ® Kids Can Read is a registered trademark of Kids Can Press Ltd.

Text © 1996 Deborah Hodge
Illustrations © 1996 Pat Stephens
Revised edition © 2008

Kids Can Press acknowledges the financial support of the Government of Ontario, through the Ontario Media Development Corporation's Ontario Book Initiative; the Ontario Arts Council; the Canada Council for the Arts; and the Government of Canada, through the BPIDP, for our publishing activity.

Published in Canada by
Kids Can Press Ltd.
29 Birch Avenue
Toronto, ON M4V 1E2

Published in the U.S. by
Kids Can Press Ltd.
2250 Military Road
Tonawanda, NY 14150

www.kidscanpress.com

Adapted by David MacDonald from the book *Bears*.

Edited by Sheila Barry and Samantha Swenson
Designed by Kathleen Gray

Printed and bound in Singapore

The hardcover edition of this book is smyth sewn casebound.
The paperback edition of this book is limp sewn with a drawn-on cover.

CM 08 0 9 8 7 6 5 4 3 2 1
CM PA 08 0 9 8 7 6 5 4 3 2 1

Library and Archives Canada Cataloguing in Publication

Hodge, Deborah
    Looking at bears / Deborah Hodge ; illustrated by Pat Stephens. —Revised ed.

(Kids Can read)
Previously published under title: Bears.
Ages 5 to 6.

ISBN 978-1-55453-249-0 (bound).   ISBN 978-1-55453-250-6 (pbk.)

1. Bears—Juvenile literature. I. Stephens, Pat, 1950– II. Title.
III. Series: Kids Can Read (Toronto, Ont.)

QL737.C27H64 2008   j599.74'446   C2007-905244-4

Kids Can Press is a *f©rus*™ Entertainment company